# A Bug on My Bed!

By Cameron Macintosh

T0360223

I can not nap.

It is not fun.

A bug is on my bed!

It is big!

I get up.

I go and get a cup.

I can not get the bug
in the cup.

I go and get a jug.

# Get in the jug, bug!

Mum and I go to the pit.

Mum tips the bug
in the mud.

The bug is in the mud.

And I am in bed!

# CHECKING FOR MEANING

1.  Why couldn't the girl in the story go to sleep? *(Literal)*

2.  What did the girl do first to try to catch the bug? *(Literal)*

3.  Why did Mum take the bug outside and put it in the mud? *(Inferential)*

# EXTENDING VOCABULARY

| | |
|---|---|
| **bug** | What is a *bug*? What is another name for a bug? What are the three sounds in this word? |
| **bed** | Look at the word *bed*. What word would you make if you added an *s* to the end of *bed*? How would this change the meaning? |
| **jug** | What is a *jug*? What do you use it for? What sounds are in this word? What other word in the story rhymes with *jug*? |

## MOVING BEYOND THE TEXT

1. Why do you think the girl was having a nap during the day?

2. How do you think the bug got into the house?

3. How would you have tried to catch the bug?

4. What would the bug eat when it is outside in the mud?

## SPEED SOUNDS

| | | | | |
|---|---|---|---|---|
| Dd | Jj | Oo | Gg | Uu |

| | | | | | | |
|---|---|---|---|---|---|---|
| Cc | Bb | Rr | Ee | Ff | Hh | Nn |

| | | | | |
|---|---|---|---|---|
| Mm | Ss | Aa | Pp | Ii | Tt |

# PRACTICE WORDS

fun

bug

bed

big

Get

Mum

get

and

up

jug

mud

cup

not

And